ALL ABOUT BEER

ALL ABOUT BEER

JOHN PORTER

Doubleday & Company, Inc.
Garden City, New York
1975

Library of Congress Cataloging in Publication Data

Porter, John H.   1918–
   All about beer.

   1. Beer.   2. Brewing.   I. Title.
TP577.P63   641.2'3
ISBN 0-385-01885-1
Library of Congress Catalog Card Number 73–20525

CONTENTS

Give me a woman who truly loves beer, and I will conquer
the world.

KAISER WILHELM

To Ellie, Janice, Jeanie, Lina, Lisa, Pat, Roberta, Sally.
We didn't conquer the world—but we had a lot of fun!

INTRODUCTION

I HAVE OFTEN WONDERED why most books have an introduction. I mean why not just get right to the thing the reader bought the book for in the first place? Maybe I do know why: it's an acceptable place for the author to talk about himself and some of his reasons for writing the book.

He suspects, of course, that probably not too many people read introductions; but that is not likely to deter him from having his little say in print. This author is no exception: he will not refrain from telling you how he came to write a book on beer.

Many years ago, when it was perhaps more common, if less fashionable, I dropped out of high school and took to hanging around the house. I had no idea of what I wanted to do, other than reading Zane Grey and Aldous Huxley and considering whether to take up cowboying or the writing of brilliant novels.

My father, unimpressed by the catholicity of this literary taste, had a third idea: Get the kid out of the house, and give him a trade. Quickly! And since Father was sales manager for a large New York brewery, things did move with terrible speed. Within ten days I had been sold into bondage— apprenticed to the trade (profession?) of brewmaster and packed off to a Manhattan boardinghouse not three blocks from a monstrous brewery: Jacob Ruppert's Knickerbocker beer. Here, I was to scrub, with a brush larger than myself, great tanks and copper kettles, using a cleanser composed of coal ashes, vitriol, and yeast. After a year of servitude I could apply for admission to the United States Brewer's Academy, where a crash course was given in organic chemistry, brewery engineering, and other fun things.

A brewery has two basic climatic conditions: very hot and humid, or very cold and humid. Also, it stinks horribly of cooking malt and hops. Moreover, the majority of brewery workers have much in common with the guards of Dachau with respect to temperament and, especially, rude humor. The general atmosphere was not congenial to my delicate spirit and physique.

I ran away twice—each time toward the golden West. The second time I made it as far as Zanesville, Ohio (a poetic coincidence?), where my treacherous secondhand Ford cashed in its last chips.

With spirit now broken, I returned to the brewery, completed the odious apprenticeship, and went on to become the youngest graduate of the academy. With the beery revels of the graduation exercises behind, I found uneasy employment as an assistant brewmaster in Pennsylvania. The advent of World War II I considered a reprieve. After the war, beer became only a hobby; much more enjoyable that way, though I still have a slight allergy to hops.

And now that time has mellowed my reaction to breweries, I realize that we made an honest and wholesome product with great skill and dedication—as much as any vintner or distiller. So why shouldn't it remain that way and be fully appreciated for the superb beverage that it is, when produced by a brewer of integrity? It is a part of the purpose of this book, then, to let beer drinkers know what good beer is all about and so, perhaps, help to maintain the tradition of fine brewing in America. There's nothing like a well-informed consumer to keep the supplier on his toes. Prosit!

ALL ABOUT BEER

1

BEER—FROM MESOPOTAMIA TO THE CLYDESDALES

IF THE DOG IS MAN'S BEST FRIEND, beer is probably his old-est. . . . And many have laid claim to being its originator. The January 1972 edition of the U.S.S.R. publication *Solsia-listichekaya Industria* asserts that the Russians invented the great refresher. While the question is unlikely to become number one on the agenda of a summit conference, it is worth noting that the first recipe for the "wine of grain" was

Fragment of an ancient Mesopotamian tablet showing a cuneiform recipe for brewing beer. The Metropolitan Museum of Art: Funds from various donors, 1886.

inscribed on stone tablets in Mesopotamia about seven thousand years before Jesus Christ elevated the wine of the grape to spiritual status; and it is known that by 1800 B.C. the Babylonians were already brewing up a storm. Next came the

Monument of the Syrian soldier, Terrura, time of Amenophis IV, with his son and his Egyptian wife, sipping beer through a cane, about 1350 B.C. Bettmann Archive.

Egyptians—frescoes and engravings on the pyramids depict the labors of brewers—who were given to believe that beer was a gift of the god Osiris or his wife, Isis. In any case, beer was the national drink of Egypt, and the Pharaohs were quick to grab a piece of the action; they cornered the barley market, owned breweries, and levied taxes on beer. (Presumably, they exempted the product of their own breweries from taxation.) The laws that governed the use of beer would put a gleam in the eye of an IRS agent. Tax-evading tavern keepers were executed by drowning, and fallen priestesses who had become pub owners took great pains in filing their returns: their penalty for hoodwinking the tax collector was burial—alive.

The practice of medicine in old Egypt was, if not scientific, at least pleasant; great curative powers were attributed to the wine of the grain. The doctors, perhaps on orders from the Pharaohs, usually prescribed beer as a sure cure for scorpion bite. If the victim did not survive, his departure from this vale had some of the zing of a sailing party aboard the *Queen Elizabeth*. A medical manual dated 1600 B.C. further attests to the merciful bent of Egyptian physicians: "a delicious remedy against death—half an onion in beer foam." If nothing else, the patient could be sure that the Angel of Death would not approach from the downwind side.

BREWING WITH BARLEY COMES TO EUROPE

APPARENTLY THE GREEKS GOT BARLEY FIRST, a fringe benefit from their forays into Egypt. They had made a sort of beer from grains, but the Egyptians were already "malting" their barley as we do today. Malting is a process of germination and heat treatment by which barley is rendered more suitable for brewing beer and ale, as we know them today. The Romans picked up the process from the Greeks, as they did so many other nice things. Then, historians suggest, beer went north with Julius Caesar's legions—about 55 B.C.—to Gaul and Britain. (There is no direct evidence of beer-brewing in Britain prior to the Roman occupation.) The Teutonic and Celtic tribes, however, had made a potable smasher from corn and honey, similar to mead, and long before the Christian era. We could call mead a beer if we wanted to, but technically and historically the term didn't come into common use until hops were added. The first use of hops is generally attributed to the monasteries of Northern Gaul, and apparently the Gaulish monks applied the Celtic word *beor* to their con-

coction. Hops were not then an absolutely essential constituent (nor are they now); they were added only to impart
a delicate bitterness to an otherwise rather sweetish drink. The
hop plant is dioecious: a fancy way of saying the male and
female reproductive organs are on separate plants. Today, only
the female "blossom" is used in brewing, *provided* it has
not been fertilized by the male, which makes it very bitter,
indeed! In fact, the male plant is banned from many European
countries. Not, we trust, a bitter augury for male humans.

During the early Middle Ages the brewing was done in
the households, mostly by women. Naturally, there had to
be a word for them, so the feminine form of brewer was

brewster. And if the ladies performed the task of converting the barley to malt by the original process of sprouting the seeds and then grinding them, they were called maltsters for their trouble. (And if they also cured hams? We have no records to tell us.) What with the names they were called, and all the hard work of cooking up the family tranquilizer, the brewsters must have been greatly relieved when the monasteries began to take over the brewing of beer. Later, these were displaced by commercial breweries. One of the first was the Weihenstepan Brewery in Freising, West Germany. Founded in the year 1040, it is said to be the oldest brewery in Europe.

THE SEAGOING BREWERS

"FROM THE FURY OF THE NORMANS, deliver us, O Lord!" This invocation expressed fear of the Vikings (then called Normans: North Men) who once sailed down from the North in warships called *drakkars* to pillage Ireland, Scotland, and the Low Countries of Europe. These amiable voyagers were as much afloat on beer as on the waters, and took no risk of running dry.

The carved and painted *drakkars*—some as long as twenty-four meters—carried bronze-bound casks of the heartening brew, as well as all necessary pots, kettles, and grains for making beer at sea. The Vikings' "loving cup" was often the horn of a cow; a forerunner, in a sense, of the Coke bottle. For wherever these Peace Corps delegates went, they left behind an appetite for the horn of beer, and enough of their brewing technology to get the natives started on their own local franchises. Of course, where they decided to colonize, they monopolized the beer trade themselves.

BEER HAD ANCESTORS ON THE MAYFLOWER

IT IS REPORTED that the Pilgrims chose to land at Plymouth Rock because they were in a super-sweat to replenish their stocks of ale. (In actuality, they called it *beere;* there is a technical difference between ale and beer, which we will go into later.) Perhaps they didn't brew at sea, as the Vikings did, because their stomachs were weaker: the smells of beer being brewed are enough to keep you hung over the rail for an entire voyage. Whether or not that was the case, these early immigrants didn't like being out of beer and apparently got to work on a batch at the first opportunity. No doubt puritanism breeds a considerable thirst.

Puritans arriving in the New World at Christmas time drinking beer on board the Mayflower. Bettmann Archive.

But the well-recorded history of brewing in America begins in 1548 when the British brewed a beer from corn during their first attempt to colonize Virginia. But "civilize" might be a better word; for then, as now, beer was considered a drink of moderation, and governments have usually encouraged its consumption on the premise that citizens are less likely to be troublesome on the malt brew than on the hard stuff. In Massachusetts (1685) they did their best to make beer available to the common man by putting a price ceiling on it. And to make it more tasty, they fined malters who turned out an inferior product. Up in Canada, Jean Talon, governor of New France, tried to solve the problem of alcoholism among his colonists by establishing the first Canadian brewery in

Budweiser—English hunting-scene tray, c. 1915. Anheuser-Busch, Inc.

Quebec city. But as far as history informs us, there were some pretty potent brews around, and the citizens who drank them had vast capacities. The man who *wants* to get smashed finds room, somewhere.

Our Founding Fathers Hoisted a Few

IN 1638 WILLIAM PENN erected the first brewery in Pennsylvania, and in the following century many men of high principle got involved with beer. The "Father of the Revolution," Samuel Adams, was a brewer, as was his father before him. Thomas Chittenden, the first governor of Vermont, was both an innkeeper and a brewer (which is really getting it both ways). And George Washington, who needs no introduction, had a very nice little brewery at Mount Vernon. Patrick Henry, Thomas Jefferson, and James Madison are described in the Encyclopaedia Britannica as men who "fostered the brewing industry."

Men of considerably less patriotism were attracted to beer in later years for reasons less than praiseworthy, e.g., Al Capone, Legs Diamond, and others who exploited Prohibition for enormous personal profits, whilst cornering the market in submachine guns and wholesale bump-offs. Theoretically, Prohibition was enacted to aid the war effort (World War I), but in fact the law didn't become effective until after the war was over. Even then, the brewing didn't stop. Some brewers made so-called near beer, which was supposed to be real beer, but with most of the alcohol removed. Sometimes it was, but since they also were allowed to make medicinal alcohol, the near beer was often "needled" by the gangsters, who got their hands on the juice by acquiring control of the breweries—using the subtle means of scaring the hell out of their owners

if crossing their palms with silver didn't work. Such games
were made possible by the fact that the lawmakers hadn't
provided funds for a policing organization when the Eighteenth Amendment was pushed through—to the considerable
surprise of the brewers, whose efforts at opposition were as
stupid as they were immense. The history of this effort was
revealed by an investigation made by a Senate committee in
the fall of 1918.

By their own admission the brewers poured money into
selected states to win elections for friends of their cause, who
promptly failed them; they financed a dummy chamber of
commerce which existed mostly for the purpose of fighting
liquor legislation; they hired experts who were to reveal the
strategy of the prohibition movement at a time when the
strategy was being revealed through every mass medium; they
even compiled a blacklist system which threatened to withhold
trade from businesses regarded as unfriendly to brewers' in-
terests. The Heinz Pickle Company—among many others—
made the honor list because its president was an officer of a
Sunday school association which had supported the cause of
Prohibition.

Examples of crude and petty attempts to block legislation
are almost endless, but eventually the brewers smartened up—
about ten years too late. When, by 1916, they deviously ac-
knowledged through advertisements in the public press that
they lamented the "false mental association" which had cou-
pled their good name with the worst of the saloons (they
owned, or controlled, almost all saloons), that issue was coming to the end of its majority. By June of 1917 American
troops were on their way to France, and the brewers had
become vulnerable to their opponents on a new set of counts:
they consumed huge quantities of grain which otherwise
would go into food; they employed a labor force which

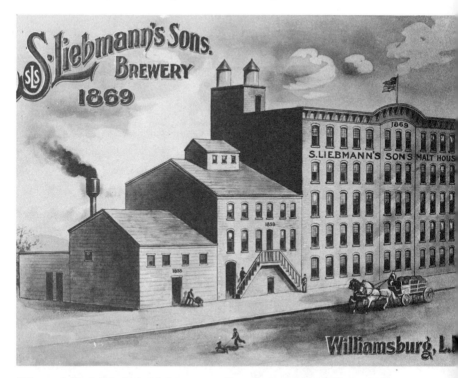

The original Rheingold brewery. See dates on buildings for growth of beer in U.S. Rheingold Brewery.

should be doing war work; and beer encouraged frivolity at a time of national crisis. Worst of all, perhaps, the brewers were Germans! Well, most of them had German names.

It had to happen, then. And what made it almost a push-over was that the attention of the press and, therefore, the public was centered on the war news while things were happening in the Congress. On January 8, 1918, four months after the Congress had finally acted, the first state ratified the Eighteenth Amendment to the Constitution. That state was Mississippi. Surprised?

An earlier trauma in the brewing industry took place

Beer being dumped into Lake Michigan, 1919. Too good for the fish. United Press International Photo.

around the middle of the nineteenth century. If less severe than Prohibition, it changed the situation quite radically in all but the New England states: what happened was that new German methods of brewing lager beer had been introduced to the United States, and the lighter brew was already catching on in places like Newark, New Jersey, which had been predominantly ale country. In 1871, P. Ballantine & Sons had just built a second ale brewery there, and they had the market pretty well sewed up with their high grades of ales, porter, and particularly "India Pale" and old stock ale. Toward the

Ballantine brewery. Ballantine.

end of the decade, Peter Ballantine, by then in his eighties, convinced his sons that it was high time to get into the beer business. The old trend-setter lived to see the new lager beer brewery completed, in 1882 (he died one year after his son, Peter H. Ballantine—in 1883).

And so Ballantine continued to prosper for the next eight decades, brewing both ale and beer, including even their unique India Pale, a brew modeled after the ale the British used to ship out to the chaps in India during the happier days of the empire. It was made strong to survive the sea voyage and the tropical climate, and Ballantine was faithful to that tradition. You can still find their India Pale in stores that cater to discriminating quaffers, but you'd better look soon. Here's why.

CREEPING MEDIOCRITY

WHAT HAS HAPPENED is that a big Midwestern brewery gobbler, Falstaff, bought Ballantine out a few years ago. And although India Pale is still being brewed—apparently under the old formula—we know what happens to products that aren't big sellers, no matter how fine they are.

It would be sad, indeed, to see our last brew of great character phased out; but that's the game of mass marketing. It may be that a bigger brewery gobbler will get Falstaff someday, or even that antitrust action will eventually be taken against the overzealous marketeers; but meanwhile there's probably only one thing we can do: drink a little less, and enjoy it more. That means making one bottle of the good imported or American stuff take the place of two cans of Old Mediocrity. Wouldn't you rather smoke one Havana cigar than a box of White Owls? Well, maybe you wouldn't.

While we're on the subject of brewery gobbling, it is only fair to point out that Falstaff has not shut down the competitors it bought out, which includes Krueger and Narragansett in addition to Ballantine, nor made any discernible changes in the products (except briefly, in the case of Ballantine ale). When a shutdown does occur, it is apt to be a small brewery in a small town—and it's tough, because the trade of the brewery worker is quite specialized; he doesn't find other employment easily at comparable wages.

The small breweries, of course, are relatively inefficient from an economic standpoint, which makes them sitting ducks for the big boys. Literally hundreds of them have been forced out of business, by fair means or foul, during the last four decades. In one case the consequences were tragic: when the Dubois Budweiser Brewery in Dubois, Pennsylvania, was bought out by a large brewery and then shut down as inefficient, the suicide rate in Dubois caught up with and surpassed the national average. While it might be difficult to prove the existence of a cause-and-effect relationship, and you probably couldn't do much about it if you did, that "coincidence" did occur in Dubois.

2

BEERS FROM ABROAD—ARE THEY WORTH THE PRICE?

ASK THE MAN who has just plunked down a dollar, or more, for a bottle of imported beer why he did it, and he feels compelled to give you a few "rational" reasons: "I don't know. I like it, I guess. . . . It has character, or something. I mean they don't rush it like we do."

He's on safe enough ground with these, and of course he isn't too eager to admit that he might have been influenced by classy advertising, elegant packaging—even by the implication that a bit of status is conferred by the word "imported" on the fancy label. One big brewer had a hunch about the status thing; he underwrote a survey at a large university. The results confirmed his worst fears: Among the various criteria students applied in forming personality judgments about one another, a preference for imported beer turned up consistently as one among a number of indicators of a "discriminating character." In short, the student who sipped the imported stuff had snatched at least one point away from the clod who guzzled the home product.

If that seems a trifle bizarre, how about this for a quaint attitude toward the beverage from across the seas? Overheard at an English-style inn in the Berkshires of Massachusetts: "I always top off an evening of gin martinis and cognac with a couple of Heinekens. . . . Never have a hangover . . . better than Alka-Seltzer!" That this epicure may, in good time, develop a liver like a medicine ball has apparently not occurred to him.

ARE IMPORTED BEERS BETTER?

IT'S TRICKY TO DEFINE "better" when the final arbiter is your own acquired taste, and taste is mostly what it's all about. But if we talk about brewing methods, quality, and kinds of ingredients, then European beer *should* taste better—at least by European taste standards.

One oversimple example points up a major difference between continental beers and their domestic counterparts. The finest hops in the world—most delicate flavor, without bitter aftertaste—come from Czechoslovakia. Those American brewers who try harder may use a small percentage of these hops, and the remainder would come from California or Oregon. Some don't use any hop blossoms at all, but a syrup extract of the domestic variety. The money they save very likely goes into advertising, which has to be pretty damn good to compensate for the inferior flavor.

Then, there's the tender business of putting the bubbles into the beer. The Old World way is to allow the beer to carbonate itself naturally during a leisurely secondary fermentation in the cold storage cellars; this tends to bind the carbonic acid gas—itself a natural product of fermentation—into the beer in very tiny bubbles. Result: a smooth, nongassy joy to mouth and stomach. The quicker New World way is to pump the gas into the beer shortly before bottling, thereby short-cutting much of the storage period. The U.S. public, long conditioned to vapid, highly charged soft drinks, swallows the often burpy mixture with understandable tolerance; for dropping an hour's wages on an imported six-pack can soon add up to the amount of the monthly car payment.

Barley malt, a classic ingredient of continental beers, is another major factor in the difference between ours and theirs. It imparts flavor, head, body (in the form of malto-dextrins and protein)—and color. The true bock and other dark beers derive their hue from the heat treatment which barley undergoes in the malting process; *not* from a prepared syrup containing caramelized sugar. But properly malted barley is expensive, and not always suitable for brewing very pale beers. Moreover, there are cheaper materials available which can supply some of the sugar needed by the yeast cells to produce that one splendid substance—ethyl alcohol—without which there would be little reason to drink the best beer in the world. The euphemism applied to these high-starch materials is "malt adjunct," as opposed to malt substitutes, which has a slightly sneaky sound to it. Malt adjuncts can be corn (maize), rice, unmalted barley, malt syrups, and tapioca starch. Corn is the commonest, while rice is used particularly for the palest beers. To the possible dismay of penurious brewers, these adjuncts won't produce the fermentable sugars without the help of the amyolytic enzymes supplied by malt. As you might have guessed, European brewers are less fond of using adjuncts—10 to 25 per cent. In the United States up to 40 per cent. But then the American brewers have several problems which are less common in Europe. One is that American

Anheuser-Busch Brewing Association uses NO CORN. Anheuser-Bush Brewing Association.

beer drinkers deep-freeze their beer (if they tasted it a bit warmer, they probably couldn't stand very much of it). The protein and other solids in high malt beers tend to come out of solution and cloud the nectar when it is overchilled. And we all know that no true American will drink anything that isn't at least twice as sparkling clear as his conscience. Also, we know how everything has got to have shelf life, and no bottled or canned beer is improved by age, light, or air. It's safer, then, to market a "thinner" beer. The trouble is that it often comes out too thin, after the final sharp filtration, and won't hold a decent head for more than ten seconds. The slippery solution to this problem is to add something to increase the "viscosity": gum arabic or some other U.S.-certified veg-gum. With the spread of American marketing techniques to the far corners of the world, we may someday see the great European breweries succumbing to these practices. But it won't be soon in Munich, where by law they must use malt alone.

ARE WE SO AWFUL?

THE PURISTS MIGHT THINK WE ARE. But most U.S. brewers are convinced that they are giving us precisely what we want (or what we have been *conditioned* to want). But so was Detroit, until the VW and the Mercedes came to our shores. Which is to say that we may not have known what we wanted until we had a wider basis for comparison. Here's a very tentative indication from out of old Chicago of how we might react if given more opportunities for choice.

Mike Royko, beer buff and feature writer for the Chicago *Daily News*, conducted and then published the results of a beer-tasting session under the headline "Suds Soakers Sink Beer

Superclaims." If not the all-time definitive study, it could at least be a shaft of barley in the wind. Eleven citizens, whose ethnicity ranged from German to Polish to Irish to Norwegian to Jewish to WASP, tested twenty-two beers and one ale in unmarked glasses. Out of a possible 55 points, the upper nine scored in this order:

> Wurzburger (Germany): 45.5
> Bass ale (England): 45
> Point Special (Wisconsin, U.S.A.): 45
> Heineken (Netherlands): 36.5
> Zywiec (Poland): 34.5
> Löwenbräu (Germany): 29.5
> Huber Premium (Wisconsin, U.S.A.): 29.5
> Kirin (Japan): 29
> Stroh's (Detroit, U.S.A.): 26

Mr. Royko points out that the Pilsner Urquell, which rated only 23, looked as though it had been on the shelf since the treaty of Versailles was signed. It probably had. He goes on to say that the two lowest ranking beers were from two of the three American giants. Or, as he put it, "the two biggest TV braggarts!"

But what is heartwarming, as well as sad, is that the Wisconsin beers that did so well probably belong to an endangered species. *Newsweek* magazine has pointed out that there were 750 breweries in the United States in 1933. Now there are only 64, and they're going fast in the face of super-heavy competition and some rather unsporting practices like price-cutting from the big three. And this in spite of beer consumption going from 40 million barrels annually to 133 million over the past forty years. "Quantitative Colossalism," as Sorokin of Harvard once called it: quantity up; quality down! Which puts many of us in the dire necessity of spending a lot of time searching for those rare products of true integrity.

What About "Export" Beers?

THESE ARE VERY OFTEN BREWED specially for export, as the word on the label implies, and in many cases even when the label doesn't specify it. Again, it's a concession to that great emasculator, shelf life. Some brewers take a chance and export the home product; those who don't, emulate some of the American brewing techniques using a higher percentage of malt adjuncts and sharp filtration; but less often do they fudge on proper aging and natural carbonation. If you do find a cloudy bottle of imported beer or ale, it's most apt to mean overchilling, or perhaps too long on the shelf; just pretend you're back in the Gay Nineties and enjoy it. If, however, it tastes sour or flat, you have a legitimate gripe (verbal only). It won't poison you.

With more beers coming from overseas, some obscure (to us) brands are turning up. Some are relatively inexpensive, which may mean they're trying to crack the U.S. market; it doesn't necessarily mean that they are inferior. The only thing to do is to try them: you may find a real bargain. That goes for U.S. beers, too.

3

THE ENJOYMENT OF BEER

To REALLY ENJOY BEER—EXPERIMENT! You don't eat the same food at every meal; your taste changes with your mood, the season, the time of day. As with food, so also with beer: brand loyalty is largely a Madison Avenue plot to make you a consistent, predictable consumer of one product.

Thousands of years of trial and error lie behind the noble brews which now await the beer drinker who is flexible enough to cultivate some fresh tastes. A little knowledge of the various types and nationalities now available in most urban areas of the United States can double your pleasure.

Lager, Ale, Pilsner: What's the Difference?

THEY'RE ALL BEER, if you go by the rather general definitions of most dictionaries. One such refers to ale as a dark, bitter beer. But by strict American definition, ale is ale, and beer is beer! The main difference stems from the species of yeast employed for fermentation. Ale yeast works better in a warm cellar, rises to the top of the vat during fermentation, and imparts the distinctive ale "tang" to the brew. Generally, it produces a slightly higher alcoholic content. In some cases it will be noticeably higher: Watney's Stingo ale (London), which comes in a small brown bottle, will knock you right off your stool if you drink it as casually as you would the average beer. It is aptly called "the poor man's whiskey" and is about the color of Bourbon.

In England today ale is synonymous in meaning with beer. Yet until the latter part of the seventeenth century, ale meant a brew made with malt, yeast, and water alone; beer was a malt brew in which hops also had been used. Since that time, the distinction has no longer applied, except insofar as the term ale is not used to describe "black beers" (porter and stout) or so-called lager beer. Lager means "storage" in German— nothing else. Rather a meaningless term, since all ales and beers are supposed to undergo some storage, at least.

The Old English ale was a mighty potent liquor, and until the fifteenth century, when beer was introduced by continental brewers, it had no rival. Perhaps Stingo is fairly close to

The obliging barmaid. "Do you like it mild, sir?" c. 1820.
Bettmann Archive.

being the modern counterpart. Friar Tuck would probably
approve of it. And nut-brown it is.

Pale ale, light-colored, with an incisive hop flavor, was
evolved at Burton upon Trent in the eighteenth century.
Bass ale originated there, and it is said that when they tried
to move the brewery and ferment the ale in new vats, they
couldn't duplicate the original flavor. Some unidentified organism in the old wood had been producing that special "zing"
during a quiet secondary fermentation. Generally, the dark-

colored ales are stronger than the light ones. Something to remember if you're ever caught short of cash in England, or for that matter in Sheffield, Massachusetts, where the Stage Coach Inn carries a good stock of London ales and beers—and some are even on draft!

If it's only clout you're looking for, at a reasonable price, then a six-pack of malt liquor is the most readily available clouter. The alcoholic content runs from 5 per cent to as high as 9 per cent by weight. It is somewhat similar to "stock" ale, which many New England bars dispensed from small kegs for several years following the repeal of Prohibition. In fact, you could hardly find anything *but* ale in the Northeastern states during that period. A legacy, no doubt, from our swinging Pilgrim forefathers.

English ales, beers, and stouts at the Stage Coach Hill Inn, Sheffield, Massachusetts. Photo by Walter Scott.

Pilsner, one of the greatest generic beer titles, originated with the brew from Pilsen, Czechoslovakia—Pilsner Urquell. It has been brewed there since 1295, perhaps earlier. They ferment it in oak casks and store it in six miles of limestone caves under the town; it takes about six months to produce a batch. The Germans import large quantities of Pilsner Urquell and also brew a similar beer called Dortmund. Both are pale, light, without being thin, slightly "hoppy" and relatively bubbly; but never gaseous. They are the true champagnes of beer. Americans brew Pilsner-type beers, almost exclusively —and sometimes come quite close to the genuine. The Scandinavians, French, Belgians, and Alsatians make some excellent Pilsners. Most Pilsners, domestic and imported, have an alcohol content of 3.5 to 4.0 per cent by weight.

Two beer types rarely seen in the United States are Vienna and Munich. Vienna is amber in color, with a very mild hop taste. The Munich types are dark brown, full-bodied, sweet, and malty. Both of these beers have alcohol contents ranging from 3 to 5 per cent.

Bock is close to the Munich type, if genuine, and is thought to have originated in Einbeck, Germany. Einbeck has been confused with *ein Bock* ("a goat"); but there are no goats in bock beer. By tradition, bock is brewed in winter for consumption in the spring; it may have added more than a little to the goatish pranks of the fertility rites of that season.

Stout, first brewed in the British Isles around the end of the seventeenth century, is by definition a beer—as is porter, which seems to have been the invention of French nuns. Both are heavy "black beers" and are considered to be high in nutritive value. Guinness used to have a solid sediment of yeast in the bottom of the bottle, and porter may contain honey and/or licorice. Both are prescribed as tonics in Europe; it is legal to imply this in the advertising—outside of the

Coors' Golden Bock. Adolph Coors Company.

United States. If you listen to the radio around St. Kitts, W.I., you will be heartened to hear a fine West Indies voice lifted in praise of stout: "You feel like a chompion with Guinness in your hond!" And indeed you may, with an alcohol content of about 5 per cent to buoy you up. Guinness also makes a superb light beer, called Harp. Not bitter, and the ladies love it! It is now imported to the United States.

Milk stout, a milder brew, seems to take its name from the fact that it is sometimes mixed, half and half, with milk. Not usually found on reducing diets, but a specific for those in a fragile condition.

Mexican and Japanese beers are usually Pilsner types. The Japanese beers are not, as is commonly believed, strictly "rice beers," but may contain a high percentage of that adjunct. The beers of these nations are generally quite light and of a very pleasant character. Sadly, they're not easy to find east of the Mississippi.

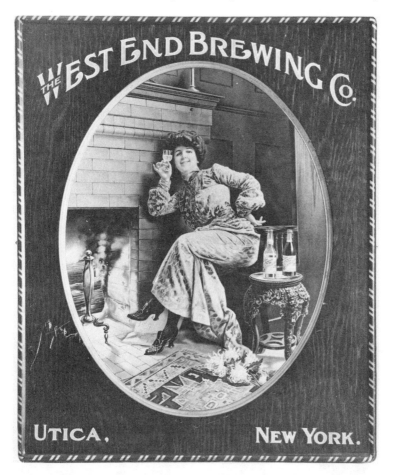

To the Ladies—West End Brewing Company. Utica Club of the West End Brewing Company.

A RESPECTFUL NOTE TO THE LADIES

KAISER WILHELM IS REPORTED TO HAVE ONCE SAID: "Give me a woman who truly loves beer, and I will conquer the world." A one-man survey isn't worth the powder to blow it to you-know-where, but it's hard to resist the temptation to take one. So for years I've been asking ladies why they drink little or no beer. The two most frequent replies are "I don't like it—it's bitter" and "I don't want to get fat!"

In answer to the last statement, you will discover in the next chapter that beer isn't quite as fattening as you have been given to believe by certain members of the soft drink axis. Moreover, you have a wide choice of light beers (and ales) to choose from—so the answer may be to hunt around a little until you find a light beer that is *not* bitter. They do exist, and they beat the socks off soft drinks on a hot day or before the fire on a frigid evening. If you can't find a domestic beer that pleases you, try to get hold of a Mexican, Danish, Irish, Japanese, or Dutch beer. These are generally light, nonbitter—and delightful!

Now, I don't suppose the following quotation will clinch

Imported beers—take your pick. Photo by Walter Scott.

my argument that you should try to get on better terms with beer, but it is another man's opinion.

"I'm not saying my men should go off on a toot right after a game, but a couple of beers puts the salt and nutriment back into the system and is far better for a pooped-out basketball player than a carbonated soft drink with all that sugar."

Danny Whelan, trainer
for the New York Knicks

4

WHAT IS THE BEER DRINKER DRINKING?

USUALLY THE BEER DRINKER IS DRINKING BEER, or a reasonable facsimile thereof. But sometimes it's *not* so reasonable, as in the case of a low-calorie beer called Gablinger's, which advertises that it contains one-third less calories. . . . Than what, we can only surmise, since regular U.S. beer runs around 160 calories per twelve-ounce bottle or can, and Gablinger's states that their brew contains just 99 calories. The point is, however, it has all the gusty deep-down goodness of a warm martini with a hair in it. At least you could get a buzz on with the martini, but you're not likely to get much out of Gablinger's because usually most of the alcohol is lost when they take out the calories. About 90 of the 160 calories in beer are in the form of alcohol. And that makes a twelve-ounce bottle of U.S. beer approximate in caloric content to a martini or an equal volume of nondietetic soda pop or Coke. Most continental beers contain about half again as much alcohol, and so a few more calories.

An average American beer of 3.5 per cent alcohol by weight is a little more than nine-tenths water. The calories not accounted for by the 90 which the alcohol represents are in the form of modest amounts of carbohydrate and protein matter. Beer may also contain traces of three members of the vitamin B complex (riboflavin, niacin, and thiamine), as well as calcium and phosphorus.

So, when all is said, beer is not quite the caloric villain that many people have been led to believe. The genuine beer belly is a rare thing these days, except occasionally among brewery workers who often are served free beer several times a day. You are not apt to get one, unless you drink it like there was no tomorrow. If sometimes you *feel* you're getting one after a bottle or two, it may well be that you're just full of gas bubbles. Try a beer that is naturally carbonated during storage. One such U.S. beer is Budweiser; another is Michelob, which is a true "premium" beer, not just a word on a can.

Hops contain substances which are chemically analogous to the female hormone, estrogen (used in the Pill). Plant physiology, a very "in" science at the moment, is discovering that many plants contain hormonelike substances which act very much like animal hormones in the human system. We might infer from this that if hops contain estrogenlike com-

The original Budweiser—for the women. Metal Budweiser advertising piece, c. 1900. Anheuser-Busch Brewing Association.

pounds, then beer could have a feminizing effect on the drinker. A pretty wild assumption, yet not utterly fantastic until disproved. But who is going to bother to do that? Certainly not a brewer's consulting laboratory. These chaps, who supplement the brewer's own lab, have a vested interest in their client's pristine image; they also supply him with additives (enzymes) used to hasten the brewing process—a perfectly harmless practice, we hasten to add.

However, in 1966 *Pageant Magazine* published an article entitled "Distinguished Doctors Name the Eight Foods That Spark Sexual Desire." Quote: "Peculiarly, of the commonly available foods, beer is most likely to give women a boost in basic femininity. . . . The hop is one of the few foods actually containing estrogens. . . ." While we certainly are not going to take *Pageant*'s word for this, we might be tempted to wonder what happens to men's basic *masculinity* when they drink a lot of beer. Probably nothing; but maybe someone should find out, if only to ease the strain on the embattled male ego. For it *is* established that a substance pres-

ent in raw wheat germ oil (an alcohol called octacosanol) has a marked effect on the physical endurance of men. This was determined by a study undertaken by the U. S. Navy in conjunction with the University of Illinois. The Navy frogmen who received the octacosanol responded, loosely speaking, as though they had been slipped a dose of male hormones: their general level of physical performance improved dramatically.

HOW ABOUT BEER'S HANGOVER QUOTIENT?

IT IS, SAD TO SAY, THE ALCOHOL that produces most of the hangover, though dull company and heavy smoking can help. But there are alcohols, and there are alcohols.

The *Wall Street Journal* published the results of a comparison study of the aftereffects of so-called hard liquors. Vodka rated lowest in hangover production, gin (not martinis) next lowest, then scotch. Bourbon was bad, and brandy was the worst. The explanation is in the *kinds* of alcohols these liquors contain. In most booze, and beer, the predominating intoxicant is ethyl alcohol, which is the simplest or "purest" from the standpoint of the drinker. Vodka, because it is highly distilled from fermented grain, comes closest to containing pure ethyl alcohol which is to say that most of the more complex "higher alcohols" have been removed during the distilling process. Medicinal alcohol is perhaps the purest of the pure ethyl alcohols (190 proof); it is on sale in Connecticut liquor stores. Some folks cut it with water to make their own vodka.

These higher alcohols, such as aldehydes, esters, and fuel oils, are the devils that contribute heavily to the morning-after syndrome. They are present in varying amounts in all natu-

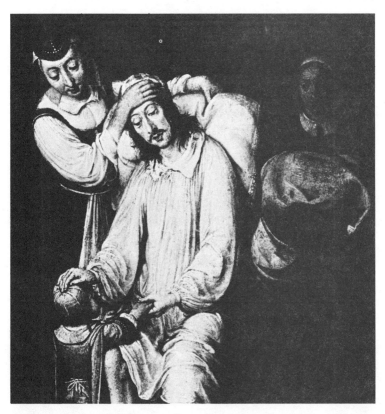

Hangover as treated by man's devoted wife with sympathy and a cooling hand, as painted by seventeenth-century artist Christian Heimbach. Bettmann Archive.

rally fermented potables, including wine, beer, and distilled spirits; they are generally absent to the degree that the spirits have been distilled. Thus, vodka is relatively free of them in comparison to beer and wine; and wine is less free of them than beer.

If you could equate the amount of beer you drink with the amount of vodka, in terms of alcohols, you could say that beer has a higher hangover quotient; but think how much beer you'd have to drink to equal the amount of alcohol in a couple of shots of straight vodka! So, for practical purposes, you needn't worry too much about those higher alcohols in beer. Not unless you're rehearsing for the lead role in *Lost Weekend*.

Draft and Bottled: What's the Difference?

Beer is delicate, like all natural products. In some ways it's as easily spoiled as milk. One of the reasons for pasteurizing milk is to increase its shelf life. Certain bacteria are inactivated, which otherwise would make the milk go sour. The same is true of beer. So canned and bottled beer are pasteurized. Draft beer, usually in barrels, is "raw." Or is supposed to be. Therefore it must be kept cold, or the live organisms it contains will go to work and change the taste. These organisms can be yeast or bacteria.

If you make beer under completely sterile conditions, or filter it *very* sharply, you may can or bottle it, and technically it's "draft" beer. Somehow it never tastes quite like the stuff that comes out of the tap in a bar. Maybe that's only mental. Or maybe the bartender doesn't keep his pipes clean, which can impart a "distinctive" taste. But on the whole, there's nothing like good beer on draft. And like many good things, it is becoming rarer because of the time and effort required in transporting and caring for it. The practice of pasteurizing bottled beer has spread to the wine industry; that includes many French wines, too! So little by little we are being weaned from the honest fruits of the earth.

BETTER NO HEAD—THAN DEAD!

When beer was made with more malts and hops than is the practice today, stability of foam was rarely a problem. Today's lighter-type lagers and ales, however, made with higher percentages of adjuncts and only mildly hopped, require assistance in maintaining an expected head of foam.

American Brewer, *December 1963*

IF THERE'S ANYTHING that panics a brewer it's pouring a glass of his own beer and seeing the head subside into about three bubbles, in nothing flat. This, of course, is because we have all learned to equate a creamy foam with Old World goodness. And rightly so. But at the same time we want our beer light, light, light! And cold, cold, cold! Thus, the American brewer finds himself between two barstools. If he makes a proper beer that has a good natural head, it may offend our effete, unlusty palates. Moreover, since it will cost him more to make, he may feel that he should be pouring that extra money into advertising and marketing his product.

A good London ale heading up as an ale should. Photo by Walter Scott.

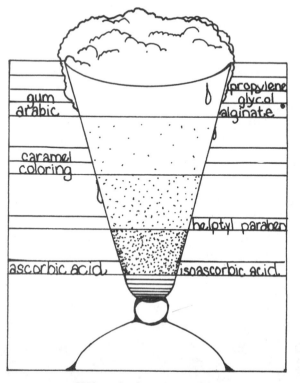

gum arabic

propylene glycol alginate

caramel coloring

heptyl paraben

ascorbic acid

isoascorbic acid

What the beer contains.

We can, therefore, *almost* sympathize when he grabs the telephone beside his glass of flat beer and dials the Kelco Company of San Diego. These beer doctors have a magic elixir that will cure his anemic beer as quickly as you can say "Prosit!" *"Even foam inhibitors cannot flatten a head that's raised with this all-but-indestructible Kelco stabilizer."* This panacea which helps to generate a photogenic, mouth-watering foam for beer commercials is modified seaweed extract, or as the brewing technologist would say, propylene glycol alginate.

It sounds worse than it is. But what of an innocent-sound-ing substance once used by brewers in Omaha, Montreal, and several other cities? This foam enhancer, tried out in the mid-1960s, was a constituent of vitamin B$_{12}$: a little goody called cobalt sulfate, as natural as motherhood. So nobody bothered to find out what happens when it is consumed with the alcohol in beer. Not until nearly fifty moderately heavy to heavy drinkers died for the sake of their beer foam. Fortunately, once the problem had been tracked down, the FDA swung into action and outlawed cobalt additives. The fact is, this was an innocent and tragic mistake, but it didn't put an end to the quest for quick-cheap additives. In 1972 a preservative called diethyl pyrocarbonate was banned because it led to the formation of urethan, a cancer-causing agent. But think of all that grand shelf life gone to waste!

A West End Brewing Company ad. Utica Club of the West End Brewing Company.

Notwithstanding the frequent reliance on chemical crutches, brewers strive to project the Old World image. In its booklet "A Story of Quality," the F. & M. Schaefer Brewing Company reassures us: "*All too often we hear about beer being made from 'chemicals.' This is a ridiculous and irresponsible statement. . . . Chemicals are never used in beer.*" Really?

It is true, thank God, that not all brewers are irresponsible; and also true that it's not necessary to use questionable additives to survive in the market. Three who fall into the responsible class, at this writing, and yet have enjoyed a modest success, are Rheingold, Budweiser, and Coors of Colorado. Coors not only lacks "chemical" additives, but has gone all the way for quality. It is aged, packaged, shipped, and stored cold; and since it is unpasteurized and contains no preservatives, it must be handled almost like milk. Being essentially a regional beer makes this possible, and Coors dominates the Southwest and has far outstripped Bud in California. But Coors is no mini-brewery: it is the fourth largest in the world and brewed 11 *million* barrels in 1973.

There are many other good brewers, of course, but we'll never know who they all are until the law which requires ingredients printed on the label is *enforced*.

5

BREWING—IS THE ART LOST?

THE ANSWER TO WHETHER THE ART of brewing is lost is yes, the *art* is lost—but not the beer. The beer is not lost, even if today brewing is a pretty exact science; there are really no secret recipes handed down from father to son. The mundane formula is: money+time+equipment+skill+talent=good beer. Great beer requires something more, a secret ingredient: the integrity of the brewer. That means he will use the best

of materials obtainable and refuse to succumb to the temptation of diverting huge sums of money to market expansion, as most of his competitors do. Nor will he pump out "green" beer to meet an unexpected demand for his product. Of course, he will probably go broke, unless he is rich enough to afford the luxury of brewing a true "premium" beer in addition to his regular product; *or* he is a small local brewer with a loyal and appreciative following, one not too responsive to the heavy pressures of advertising and price-cutting by his national competitors. But where in America do you find enough people who know, or care that much about fine beer? Well, legend has it that we were once a nation of discriminating beer drinkers, perhaps because the memory of the Old Country brews was still on our palates. And we hear a lot of prattle from the advertising agencies about modern beers that still have that old-time, deep-down goodness. Do they?

That depends on your definition of "goodness." If you mourn the loss of nutritious yeast cells floating around in the beer, or the insoluble proteins, the "live" enzymes and vitamins, the odd bits of flotsam, the changing quality of your favorite brew, and the sediment in the bottle's bottom; then you could say that the goodness is gone and you have been lied to once again. If, however, you persist in mourning, you can brew your own beer at home and get much the same beverage, in appearance, at least. But before we give you helpful hints on how to do this, you might wish to know something of how the professionals go about producing a clear, brilliant, palatable beer, *consistently*. This is not to inhibit your own efforts, but to tell you what is involved in producing one of the few "natural" products still available in packaged form.

The Brewmaster and the Brewing

What brewing is all about nowadays is to arrive at an alcoholic beverage that tastes good, looks good, keeps well, is "cheap," and is uniform in flavor year after year. No simple tricks in themselves; then add the guessing game of trying to have just enough properly aged beer on hand to meet the rather unpredictable demands of the public.

All of these, and many more, are problems of the modern brewmaster, a highly trained specialist who must also be jack

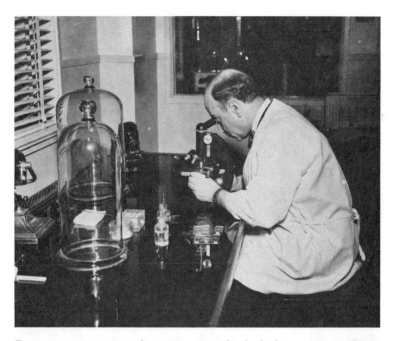

Brewmaster performing first step in isolating yeast cell for pure culture propagation. Rheingold Brewery.

of a number of trades: executive, organic chemist, engineer, biologist, and taste-tester *extraordinaire*. He may have acquired his skills at a university in Germany, a brewer's academy in the United States, or a technical college in California. And he has probably had to serve a long apprenticeship as a tank-scrubber in a brewery before going to school. In a big brewery he has several assistants, and a laboratory for which Pasteur would have sold his soul. In the laboratory he keeps pure cultures of the yeast cells which ferment his beer. Through his microscope he studies the health state of these cells and keeps a sharp watch for airborne "wild" yeasts and bacteria which would impart strange odors and tastes to his brew. Among the micro-organisms that plagued the brewmaster for centuries is one called penicillin. Little did he suspect what this pesky mold in his vats would one day mean to mankind's health!

The brewmaster works with apparently simple materials: water, yeast (a type of fungi), hops, barley malted by germination and "roasting," and sometimes other starchy ingredients. The whole idea, greatly simplified, is to give the yeast cells something good to "eat" and to metabolize, so that as they reproduce themselves they will manufacture alcohols and little bubbles of carbon dioxide. What the yeast considers good eating is a sugar called maltose. The yeast we are talking about, incidentally, is *brewers'* yeast, which belongs to the species *Saccharomyces cerevisiae*, which is Latin for "Don't try to make a decent beer with just any old yeast." There are a great many types within this single species; from the brewer's point of view they can be placed in two categories, "bottom" and "top," depending on whether the cells sink or rise during fermentation. Lager yeast sinks; ale yeast rises.

THE BREWING PROCESS

THE THREE MAIN STAGES of the brewing process are mashing, boiling, and fermentation.

Mashing methods vary, depending on the type of beer or ale being brewed, but are basically a way of converting the starches in the grains into soluble, fermentable sugars—maltose and dextrins. This is done by adding heated water to the ground grain(s). The temperature and chemical composition of the water—both strictly controlled—are what activate enzymes that convert the starches. The proteins, too, are partly modified during the mashing.

Temperature and acidity of the water at this stage are

The brewhouse and kettles—the mash tubs are on the second floor and the brew kettles are beneath. Anheuser-Busch Brewing Association.

everything to the final product. A high temperature, for example, will produce a more dextrinous but less fermentable "lunch" for the yeast and, therefore, less alcohol but a more fully flavored beer. The quick-mashing method, used in America, employs two mashes at temperatures of about 145° and 172°F. The European method usually employs four temperature stages, ranging from 100° to 170°F., which gives the proteolytic enzymes a chance to convert the proteins into more soluble states. When the mashing is finished, the resulting concoction is known as wort. It is then ready for the boiling in great copper kettles.

Boiling prevents further enzyme action and coagulates a lot of the protein material. It also sterilizes the wort and concentrates it. The degree of concentration is measured by a hydrometer (like the thing they use to check the antifreeze in your car radiator), only it is read in degrees Balling. A high-Balling wort becomes a heavy beer and, of course, is more expensive to make because it contains less water. During the boiling of the wort hops are added—poured down the huge chimneys that rise from the kettles. Hops impart the slightly

Boiling in the brewing process. Anheuser-Busch Brewing Association.

bitter flavor, but that's not all. They contain resins and oils whose derived constituents act as a preservative; their tannin helps to precipitate more of the protein, which might create a "haze" in the finished beer.

Fermentation begins after the wort has been filtered to remove the hop blossoms and other insoluble materials; then cooled. Yeast does its thing in the fermentation cellars at an optimum temperature (for lager beer) of approximately 45° F. The sooner the yeast begins to grow, the less chance for infection of the wort by mold spores, airborne bacteria, and "wild" yeasts (and you don't take any chances with hundreds of barrels of expensive wort). Modern breweries, of course, have fancy air filtration systems, so they stir it up a bit with compressed, clean air to get things going in a hurry. Within a few hours a fine, fluffy head appears on the wort; fermentation is under way. For the next seven or eight days the yeast cells are metabolizing and reproducing like mad. It has been calculated that you could cover the earth with yeast in ninety-six hours if it had enough wort to feed on. During these days of great activity the temperature must not be allowed to go much above 50°, or the yeast will go on a slowdown strike. After about eight days most of the fermentable matter will have been converted into alcohol, and we now have "green" beer, which is pumped into the storage cellars. Most of the yeast is left behind, ready to start work again on fresh wort.

The storage cellars are kept at just over 32°, and a slow secondary fermentation takes place; protein and some yeast settle out and more carbon dioxide is evolved. The beer improves in flavor—as long as oxygen is excluded. This storage phase may continue for three months; longer periods don't improve most beers. In fact, the opposite is usually the case. As you might expect, many U.S. brewers like to

Battery of glass-lined tanks for aging the beer after fermentation, which mellows the beer to full flavor. Rheingold Brewery.

shorten the storage phase. One method is to add enzymes which break down the complex proteins, and so clarify the beer in less time.

If you have ever wondered why your favorite beer tastes the same year after year, that is because many brews are blended in the storage tanks, which tends to blur distinctions among individual brews.

A note to the do-it-yourself brewer about yeast: if you want to make a good beer, consistently, bear this in mind. Pure strains of yeast have been used in bottom fermentation since this practice was introduced in 1883 by E. C. Hansen, first director of the Carlsberg laboratory in Copenhagen. Later, pure strains were mixed, e.g., one that starts fermenting quickly with one that is a good converter of sugar to ethyl alcohol. Pure-culture yeasts, these days, are carefully worked up from laboratory stocks or taken from previous, uninfected brews. The ratio of yeast to wort is roughly one pound to thirty-two gallons of wort. The thing to remember is to keep your brewers' yeast in a cool place in a sterile container.

Water, a very important ingredient in brewing, is the subject of much hot air in advertising. Individual brewers are still claiming that they have the best beer because of their pristine water supply. Long ago this was true. In fact, the suitability of the water supply determined the locations of most breweries; and different kinds of waters *are* used for the brewing of different types of beers and ales.

But today the brewer who tells you that his beer owes its superiority to the crystal spring in his backyard is pulling your leg, or both of them. The simple truth is that almost any water fit to drink can be adjusted by the addition, or modification, of natural minerals.

The critical factor in brewing water or "liquor," as the British call it, is hydrogen-ion concentration. Roughly, this corresponds to the degree of acidity as measured on the pH scale. If the water is on the alkaline side, much unwanted matter will be dissolved from the husks of the malt. Also, the activity of those magic enzymes will be diminished unless the solution is somewhat acid.

The common cause of alkalinity in water is the presence of magnesium and calcium bicarbonates in solution. This is known as temporary hardness and can be removed by boiling the water (scale in the kettle). Permanent hardness actually gives a slightly acid solution and is apt to be an advantage to the brewer. These water problems don't exist to the same degree for the home brewer, since he is usually working with malt syrup in which much of the enzymic activity has already occurred.

BARRELS, BOTTLES, AND CANS

BEFORE PROHIBITION, and for a while after Repeal, most of the beer came out of the breweries in oak barrels, or half barrels. A full barrel of beer contained thirty-one U.S. gallons and weighed about three hundred pounds; it took quite a man to stack them three high in the "racking" room where they were filled and the bung was hammered in with a mallet. The barrels of beer were transported to the saloons (often owned by the brewer himself) and dispensed from taps behind the bar. This was draft beer, and if you wanted some to take home, you "rushed the growler." Either it was given to you in a cardboard container, or you brought your own pitcher, can, or stein. Often enough, Papa sent one of the kiddies to fetch his evening tranquilizer.

But the time came when the brewers were forbidden by law to own retail outlets—could this be an omen for the oil companies?—and the marketing revolution decreed that bottles and cans would gradually displace the old oaken barrel. For a time cans were resisted by the consumer on the theory that they spoiled the taste of the beer. And glass companies did their best to support that theory. But the cans were lined with lacquer, which was chemically inert. Rarely do you encounter a bad can of beer. Probably the can is the ideal container; it admits no light, which is an enemy of beer, and there is less space for air (as in the neck of a bottle); oxygen is also bad for beer. Bottles persist in bars largely

The angel and Schlitz. Joseph E. Schlitz Brewing Company.

for aesthetic reasons; usually they are brown or green to protect the beer from light, which can produce a "skunky" taste as a result of photosynthesis. Direct sunlight is the thing to avoid. (Stay away from clear bottles of Miller High Life if it comes out of a store window.)

The Can Collectors

THE BEER CAN has come a long way since its timid beginnings when Krueger Beer, of Richmond, Virginia, test-marketed canned brew in 1934. It wasn't until 1969 that canned beer surpassed the bottled variety in annual sales.

Now the can is king, and the ranks of the Beer Can Collectors of America—formed in St. Louis, Missouri, in 1970—are swelling (swilling?) as a result. This esoteric group now has members in forty states, as well as Japan and Brazil. The BCCA holds an annual "CANvention," publishes a semimonthly news report (how would you like to be left on a desert island with only that to read?), and ranks its members according to the number and varieties of cans in their collections. Rare cans, of course, are highly prized. One of the rarest brands ever canned was Schaefer's beer, which was supplied to the military in 1942. The can was olive drab, so that soldiers could drink it on the front lines without being spotted by the enemy. Some collectors specialize in cans with animal names, like Leopard Lager and Mule Malt Liquor. Others prefer more freaky names, such as Soul Malt Liquor, brewed in Watts, California.

The King and Queen of can collectors are Mr. and Mrs. Denver Wright, Jr., of St. Louis, who have the largest collection of its kind—over one thousand cans—in the world. My, how their heirs will battle for *that* legacy!

6

HOW ABOUT HOME BREWING?

"Making Beer at Home Can Put You Over a Barrel." That's the headline on an item which appeared in the *Wall Street Journal* in August 1973. The dateline is Washington, D.C. The gist of it is that the Treasury's Bureau of Alcohol, Tobacco, and Firearms (quaint Trinity) warns us that federal law prohibits producing beer at home. The bureau notes that some home beer kits being sold claim an individual is

A risky solution to the Great Drought. New York Public Library.

allowed to make up to two hundred bottles of beer a year for personal use, but that under law beer can be made only at breweries. The bureau adds, however, that people may produce up to two hundred gallons of wine per year provided they register with the bureau before making the wine. The winos must have a friend in Washington.

Do we hear the stentorian tones of two outraged home brewers echoing down through the years—George Washington and Samuel Adams? To say nothing of many other fathers, even mothers, of our country who could not have imagined so dastardly a usurpation of our inalienable rights.

What next? A law to forbid us rolling our own cigarettes? No more homemade cookies?

The question for us is how seriously do we regard the home brewing law? If it permits the manufacture of beer kits, but not the use of them, we seem to be faced with

Home brewing.

To make Small Beer.

Take a large Sifter full of Bran
Hops to your Taste. — Boil these
3 hours then strain out 30 Gall.ᵒⁿˢ
into a cooler put in 3 Gall.ⁿˢ
Molasses while the Beer is
Scalding hoᵗ, rather draw the
Molasses into the cooler & Strain
the Beer on it while boiling Hot
let this stand till it is little more
than Blood warm then put in
a quart of Yeast if the Weather is
very cold cover it over with a Blank
& let it work in the cooler 24 hours
then put it into the Cask — leave
the Bung open till it is almost don
Working — Bottle it that day Week
it was Brewed

ambivalence, if not flagrant inconsistency. The answer, if there is one, may be to borrow from Catholic theology and say it is a matter of individual conscience. Small consolation if the revenue agents come knocking at the door. Meanwhile, some words on how home brewing should be done *if* one were permitted to do it.

HOME BREW À LA PAPA

THERE ARE TWO BASIC WAYS to make home brew: the old way, and the right way. No matter what we may *think* we remember about the great brew Papa used to make in the cellar, it was more or less vile: it usually tasted like soap

George Washington's home recipe. National Association of Brewers.

> *To make Small Beer—*
> *Take a large Siffer full of Bran*
> *Hops to your taste. —Boil these*
> *3 hours. Then strain out 30 Gall'ns*
> *into a Cooler [.] [P]ut in 3 Gall'ns*
> *Molasses while the Beer is*
> *Scalding hot or rather draw the*
> *Molasses into the Cooler & Strain*
> *the Beer on it while boiling Hot[.]*
> *[L]et this stand till it is little more*
> *than Blood Warm[.] [T]hen put in*
> *a quart of Yeast[.] [I]f the Weather*
> *is very Cold cover it over with a Blank[et]*
> *& let it Work in the Cooler 24 hours[.]*
> *[T]hen put it into the Cask—leave*
> *the Bung open till it is almost don[e]*
> *Working—Bottle it that day [a] Week*
> *[from the day] it was Brewed*

suds, spoiled quickly, and blew up in the bottles. What Papa did was what lots of people are still doing. They buy some malt syrup, add some table sugar, some water, a cake of Fleischmann's (*bakers'* yeast), and stir it around in an open crock. When they decide, largely by guess, that all the sugars have been converted to alcohol, they pour it into bottles and put on the caps. Impatiently, they wait for the beer to settle down and improve with age. Usually, it doesn't. If they try this method enough times, they may eventually produce something fit to drink, but still a long way from civilized beer.

What they should do is take some advice, invest twenty-five or thirty dollars in good equipment and the proper ingredients; then, brew a good beer the first time. The cost per bottle will work out to about five or ten cents after paying for the equipment with money saved on the first few batches. Of course, the cost will depend on the quality of beer brewed. A fair approximation of a German beer will run closer to the ten-cent figure.

The point is that within the last ten years what were once considered the exclusive secrets of the great breweries have become available to the general public: a variety of pure strains of brewers' yeast, simple control instruments like hydrometers, good hops, and, perhaps most important, corn dextrose, a form of sugar much appreciated by brewers' yeast.

HOME BREWING IN THE 1970S

IF YOU REMEMBER, the basic ingredients are malt, hops, water, and yeast. And if you want to make the beer amateurs make, you can rely on the local A&P or First National supermarket, and some others, for Blue Ribbon Pale Dry malt syrup with hop flavoring added. But you're on your own for the rest of the ingredients and they're critical, because you are dealing with some intricate biochemical happenings. So unless you want to fool around with Papa's Low-grade Lager and mess up your kitchen or cellar for nothing, heed the following instructions regarding ingredients and equipment. The name and address of a supplier is listed at the end of the chapter.

EQUIPMENT

FOR A FIVE-GALLON BATCH—the most practical for beginners—which will give you about fifty-five twelve-ounce bottles of beer, you need the following:

Primary fermentor. What works best is a large plastic pail that will hold an extra gallon or two to accommodate the froth of fermentation. Clean it first with hot water and baking soda to remove the industrial film common to polyethylene. Use a pound of soda and let it soak for several hours in five gallons of water. Rinse it well with fresh hot water.

Cover. A large sheet of plastic to put over the fermentor. This is to keep out the air. Fasten with masking tape or string.

Carboy. A carboy is a large glass bottle, often used to hold industrial acid. They also come in plastic. Five gallons is the size you want. You will use it as a *secondary* fermentor. Clean this as you did the primary fermentor.

Fermentation lock. This is also called a water seal. It fits into the top of the carboy; it permits gas to escape without allowing air to get in. A simple device.

Thermometer. Temperature control is imperative. Wort that is too hot will kill the yeast beasties. Control is especially critical if you are brewing a light lager. The thermometer you want is the immersion type that floats, in the primary fermentor. In the average home the problem is to keep the wort cool enough. You can hang a plastic bag of ice in it, or work in a cool cellar, if you have one.

Hydrometer. This instrument measures the specific gravity of liquids. The two common types are the S.G. scale and the Balling, or Brix, scale. Either type gives you a fair reading of the amount of fermentable sugar present at various stages of fermentation. Take a sample of the wort out of the fermentor in a small vessel and float the hydrometer in it. The best thing to do is buy a testing jar with the hydrometer.

Siphoning hose. You'll use this to transfer the liquid from container to container. The idea is to leave the sediment behind. Get the right kind from a brewing supplies house.

Miscellaneous items. An extra-wide box of Saran Wrap to cover the primary fermentor. (You can watch the fermentation in progress.) Masking tape. Measuring cup. Long plastic spoon for stirring the wort.

Bottles. The best type to use is the old, long-neck, twelve-ounce beer bottle; it's almost the only kind you can cap properly. They aren't easy to find nowadays, except in taverns. Your friendly pub owner will probably sell you a few cases of empties.

Capper. You may be able to get a bottle capper from your local hardware store. Otherwise, the brewer's supply house. And don't forget the bottle caps.

INGREDIENTS

IF YOU HAVE READ the foregoing sections of this book, it may have occurred to you that brewing a decent beer is somewhat more scientific than making Mulligan stew. But if you are still game to try brewing at home, and it *is* fun, then send a note off to a brewing supply house and ask them to send you a catalog. Everything mentioned here is available from the supplier listed at the end of this chapter, or from one of his forty-eight branch stores around the nation.

As an apprentice brewer, you would be well advised to start with the kind of light beer you are used to drinking, and to use the simplest method. Here's what you will need for five gallons of light Pilsner-style lager:

5 gallons water	*All-purpose dry beer yeast*
2 pounds corn sugar (dextrose)	*Yeast nutrient (vitamins)*
3 pounds dried malt extract	*1 teaspoon brewing salts*
1 4-ounce can hop extract	*½ teaspoon beer finings*
1 teaspoon salt	*1 teaspoon ascorbic acid*
1 teaspoon citric acid	*(vitamin C)*

Now, if we can assume that you have waited impatiently for your equipment and ingredients to arrive, and finally they have, what do you do first?

1. Boil the water. That's right, just like in the old Westerns when Maureen O'Hara was going to have a baby. And we do it partly for the same reason—to protect our first baby batch from infection—but also to help soften the water and drive off chlorine. If you haven't enough pots and pans, at least boil the gallon you are going to use to create the wort.

2. Now, set aside 2 cups of corn sugar for bottling. Next, put the rest of the sugar, the dried malt extract, the hop extract, salt, citric acid, and 1 gallon of hot water in the primary fermentor. Stir this mess until everything is dissolved. You now have wort!

3. Add the remainder of the water. If you haven't boiled all the water, and the remainder of the water is fairly cool, you may come out somewhere near 60° to 65° F., which is where you want to be. *Not* warmer. So you may have to use the ice bag trick. Keep the plastic cover on the fermentor as much as possible while adjusting temperature; the air in your kitchen is full of beer spoilers.

4. If you *are* in the kitchen, now is the time to lug the fermentor down to the cellar or to the coolest place in the house. The most difficult problem will be to maintain correct temperature, particularly when the wort is in the secondary phase of fermentation. That's where the commercial brewers have a marked advantage.

5. Now you can use the hydrometer. When the temperature is 60° to 65° F., specific gravity should be between 1.035 and 1.038. If you get a reading above or below these limits, adjust it. Too low, add sugar; too high, add water. In either case, add a little at a time, and stir before taking the reading. Remember to use the testing jar; don't try to float the instrument in the wort. The reason for all this messing about is that you can't be sure of the precise amount of sugar in the malt extract.

6. Add the yeast and yeast nutrient. Stir. Re-cover the fermentor and put a lightproof cloth or blanket over the Saran Wrap. Wash all your instruments thoroughly.

7. Let fermentation proceed! But don't let the temperature rise much over 65°. Keep it a bit under that if you can. After six days, or when the wort has attenuated to 1.010—

whichever comes first, as the car makers say—siphon into the secondary fermentor and add the brewing salts (more goodies for the yeast). Also add the beer finings. These may be gelatin, or better, isinglass. They help greatly to clarify the beer by causing precipitation of colloids. Don't forget to attach the fermentation lock.

8. Let the secondary fermentation continue for two weeks, or until the S.G. is 1.000. That's terminal. Ideally, the temperature should be kept between 40° and 50° F., though that's not always easy to achieve at home. It slows down the fermentation, but makes a considerable difference in the quality of the finished beer. At the proper temperature it may take three weeks to reach a S.G. of 1.000, but you are also aging the beer at the same time. It's not time lost.

9. Make a syrup, using beer, of the two cups of sugar and the ascorbic acid (an antioxidant) and stir slowly into the green beer. Siphon it back into the primary container before you do this, thereby getting rid of much sediment. If you want to cheat a little, like some of the commercial brewers, you can also add a "heading liquid" at this time. It assures a fine collar in the glass. The suppliers also provide this stuff. It's quite wholesome, *if* you stick to what the recommended supplier offers.

10. Siphon into bottles and cap. (Use brown or green bottles.)

11. Store for at least two weeks in a cool place. Drink. Put some aside for three months, and notice the difference.

A word about the yeast mystique. Not much has been said here about this, for fear of making brewing seem too complex and thus discouraging the apprentice. This much you should know. Yeast, being a living organism, needs all the pampering it can get. This means proper feeding and comfortable temperatures. When you are starting the fer-

mentation part of your brewing, you want to be sure that the
yeast is ready to swing into action and thereby discourage
such airborne bacteria as acetobacter, which can turn your
batch into vinegar in no time at all. It isn't a bad idea, then, to
make a "yeast starter" up in advance, as a precautionary
measure. Essentially, what you do is make up a little wort,
about 32 ounces, add a pinch of brewers' yeast, then put this
in a sterile bottle (64 ounces) at 70° F. In twenty-four to
forty-eight hours this can be added to the primary fermentor,
and things will get going in a hurry. You will find that
most packets of brewers' yeast carry instructions on this
simple process.

You should also know that the foregoing recipe is only
one of many. You can make ale, porter, stout, and all the
varieties of beer. There are books entirely devoted to the
brewing of these delights, also available through your supplier. For information on obtaining books and all necessary
brewing equipment and ingredients, write to:

> Wine-Art Westchester
> 91 Sawmill River Road
> Elmsford, New York 10523
>
> or for the store nearest to
> you (there are fifty-two in the United States),
>
> Wine-Art Sales Ltd.
> 3417 West Broadway
> Vancouver 8, B.C., Canada

7

YOUR BEST FRIEND IN THE KITCHEN

FOR SOME UNKNOWN REASON beer hasn't really caught on in the American kitchen. It may be that we simply haven't discovered all the things it can do for food, *and* for the cook! For example, it makes an admirable substitute for milk, water, chicken stock, beef broth, even wine, in any recipe you are now using. And you can use it for crisper batters, pancakes, soups, stews, pot roasts, and ultra-light soufflés. The subtle flavor it adds to familiar foods is different enough to make them interesting, but not so pronounced as to make conservatives and children scream with surprise. Beer doesn't dominate the flavor of the dish; it somehow enhances it.

So where's the catch? Of course, it's got to be fattening. Not so you would notice. A cup of beer has a little over one hundred calories; and as we have seen, nearly half of those calories are in the alcohol, which evaporates in the cooking. So you're going to end up with a lot less than if you used milk or chicken stock.

What kind of beer is best for cooking? Generally speaking, the beer you like to drink. But even if you don't like beer, you still won't find it objectionable in most recipes; it almost ceases to be beer after the cooking. There is one thing to be said about the kind of beer to use: You may find the American beers a little too light to compete with dishes that contain strong-flavored foods like onions, garlic, even beef. In that case use a dark beer, like bock or a Munich type. With seafoods try a good ale: LeBatt, Ballantine, or Bass; but use the latter sparingly. And if you are a true beer buff, drink the same beer or ale with the meal. Pour it into a tall Pilsner glass or a goblet; pour it in a way that puts as much head on it as you want. Just be sure the glasses have no soap or milk film on them (wash them with detergent); there should be no tiny bubbles sticking to the inside of the glass; that means the glass is dirty, and the beer will tend to go flat. As for the temperature of the beer, most American beers taste best when they're too cold to taste—around forty-two degrees. The European beers are at their best about ten degrees warmer.

Before some delicious recipes using beer and ale, here are some classic potions with beer, stout, and ale bases.

Bottle-shaped cork pull. Anheuser-Busch Brewing Association.

SHANDYGAFF

Said to be a favorite drink of the British during colonial days in India. Wonderful with curried dishes.

1 12-ounce bottle chilled ale
1 10-ounce bottle chilled ginger ale

Gently stir ale and ginger ale in a pitcher. Serve in chilled Pilsner glasses. Makes 4 servings.

BLACK VELVET

A really tangy, yet amazingly smooth drink.

1 12-ounce bottle cold Guinness stout
1 split extra-dry chilled champagne

Stir gently in a chilled pitcher. Serve in champagne glasses. Makes 4 servings. And wow!

APRÈS SKI

To warm the cockles of your heart after skiing, or after anything else!

1 teaspoon dextrose (corn sugar), corn syrup, or simple syrup
  (sugar and water)
1 12-ounce bottle ale
Grated nutmeg

Put sugar or syrup in earthenware mug or metal tankard. Add ale. Plunge the white-hot tip of a poker into the brew. Dust the top with nutmeg. (Tradition has it that nutmeg is one of nature's natural aphrodisiacs.) Makes 1, or possibly 2 servings.

ELIZABETHAN SMASHEROO

This may have been responsible for Will Shakespeare's *Rape of Lucrece*.

4 quarts ale
½ pint gin
1 dash nutmeg
2 pinches ground ginger

Heat the ale *almost* to boiling. Add the gin after removing from stove. Stir in nutmeg and ginger. Drink out of warmed mugs. Makes servings for about 8 hearty souls.

ALE POSSET

A venerable classic for those who are feeling a trifle depleted.

10 eggs, separated
1 quart cream or half-and-half
1 tablespoon sugar
1 cup beer
1 cup ale
4 ounces scotch whiskey
Ground clove
Ground cinnamon
Grated nutmeg

Beat yolks of 10 eggs and whites of 5 with cream, adding sugar along the way. Then stir in beer, ale, and scotch. Sprinkle in clove and cinnamon to taste. Stir the posset over low heat until it thickens. Serve in warmed mugs. Sprinkle the nutmeg on top. Makes 12 servings.

HERE ARE SOME RECIPES for main dishes which include beer or ale.

RED CABBAGE WITH BEER

10 slices bacon
2 onions, chopped
2 green apples, peeled, cored, and sliced
1 small red cabbage, shredded
1 tablespoon red currant jelly
1 pinch nutmeg
½ cup beer
Salt and pepper to taste

Fry the bacon. Remove when crisp and drain on paper towels. Discard surplus bacon fat; sauté onions and apple in

Church dignitary discusses flavoring with cook in a painting by J. G. Vibert. Bettmann Archive.

remainder. Transfer to a deep casserole and add shredded cabbage, jelly, nutmeg, beer, and salt and pepper. Simmer over low heat for 1 hour. Great with pork. Serves 4.

WELSH RABBIT

½ cup beer
1 cup grated Cheddar cheese
1 teaspoon Worcestershire sauce
1 teaspoon dry English mustard
¼ cup whipping cream

Bring beer to boiling point. Add grated cheese, Worcestershire sauce, and mustard. Stir until smooth. Add cream to thin to correct spreading consistency. Spread on toast and brown under broiler. Serves 2.

BITTER BATTER SHRIMP

These shrimp can be served with cocktails, as a first course, or as a lunch dish. Choose the largest shrimps you can find and dip them into beer batter (next recipe).

16 very large shrimp, peeled and deveined
Juice of 1 lemon
1 cup flour
1 recipe Bitter Batter (below)
Parsley sprigs
Lemon wedges

Cut the shrimp down the back but keep the tail shell attached. Sprinkle shrimp with lemon juice. Dip the shrimp into flour and then into beer batter. Allow the excess batter to drain off, and deep-fry shrimp until golden brown and crisp, about five minutes at 375°. Drain and serve immediately, garnished with parsley and lemon wedges. Serves 4.

BITTER BATTER

1 12-ounce bottle beer
1 egg, slightly beaten
1 cup sifted all-purpose flour
1 teaspoon salt
1 teaspoon paprika

Combine all ingredients in a bowl, stirring with a wire whisk. Use for Bitter Batter Shrimp (above).

BEEF STEW WITH ALE

2½ pounds chuck steak
3 tablespoons oil
4 large onions, chopped
2 cloves garlic, crushed
1 tablespoon prepared mustard
2 tablespoons flour
1½ cups ale
1 bay leaf
2 sprigs parsley
¼ teaspoon peppercorns
½ teaspoon thyme
1 teaspoon salt
1 teaspoon sugar
¼ teaspoon grated nutmeg

Preheat oven to 350°. Trim beef and brown in a skillet in hot oil. Transfer beef to a casserole and brown onions in oil. Add garlic, mustard, and flour. Stir in ale and add the bouquet garni ingredients, tying them in a bag made from a small piece of cheesecloth. Add salt, sugar, and nutmeg. Pour sauce over browned beef. Cover casserole and place in the oven for 2 hours. Serves 4.

BRAISED BEEF WITH TOMATOES AND RIPE OLIVES

2½ pounds chuck steak
3 tablespoons oil
2 onions, sliced
1 green pepper, cut into thin strips
1 cup ripe olives, pitted
3 tomatoes, peeled, seeded, and quartered
1 teaspoon tomato paste
1 tablespoon flour
1½ cups ale
Salt and pepper to taste

Preheat oven to 350°. Cut beef into cubes. Trim well. Sauté in a skillet in hot oil, adding a few pieces at a time. Transfer as it browns into a casserole. Sauté onion and pepper in oil until softened. Add ripe olives, tomatoes and tomato paste and cook for 1 minute. Stir in flour and add ale slowly. Season with salt and pepper and add contents of skillet to the casserole. Cook for 2½ hours in preheated oven until tender. Serves 4 to 6.

STEAK AND KIDNEY PIE

2 pounds chuck steak, cubed
2 lamb kidneys, trimmed and chopped into small pieces
2 tablespoons oil
1 onion, chopped
2 tablespoons flour
1½ cups dark beer
1 tablespoon Worcestershire sauce
Salt and pepper to taste
Pie crust
1 bay leaf

Preheat oven to 375°. Brown steak and kidneys in hot oil in a heavy skillet, a few pieces at a time. Transfer to a casserole just large enough to hold all of the meat. Sauté onion in oil, adding a little more oil if necessary. Stir in flour and add beer gradually. Season with Worcestershire sauce and salt and pepper. Pour sauce over meat and add bay leaf. Cover and cook in the oven for 2 hours.

Raise oven temperature to 400°. Cover surface of meat in casserole with pastry crust. Bake 15 minutes until crust is set and lightly browned. Reduce oven heat to 350° and continue cooking for 25 minutes. Serve with onions boiled in bouillon. Serves 4 to 6.

STEAMED FRANKFURTERS WITH SAUERKRAUT

1 1-pound can sauerkraut
1 onion, chopped
1 apple, peeled, cored, and thinly sliced
1 cup beer
1 pound all-beef frankfurters

Drain sauerkraut. Rinse under cold running water and press dry. Place sauerkraut in saucepan. Add chopped onion, sliced apple, and beer. Simmer 30 minutes over low heat. Put frankfurters into saucepan of boiling water. Remove from the heat and leave frankfurters in water for 10 minutes. Drain and serve on top of drained sauerkraut. Serves 4.

CHICKEN LIVERS PAPRIKA

1 pound chicken livers
2 tablespoons butter
1 medium-sized onion, chopped
1 teaspoon paprika
1 tablespoon flour

1 cup beer
Juice of ½ lemon
Salt and pepper to taste
2 tablespoons cream

Sauté halved livers in butter about 3 minutes. Sauté onion until soft. Stir in paprika and flour. Add beer gradually, then the lemon juice. Season with salt and pepper and add cream. Simmer for 4 minutes. Serve on toast or rice. Serves 4.

HAM SLICES AND SAUERKRAUT

1 1-pound can sauerkraut
1 cup dark beer
2 slices smoked or boiled ham
1 tablespoon Dijon mustard
¼ cup white seedless raisins
1 tablespoon brown sugar
1 tablespoon butter
1 teaspoon cornstarch dissolved in 1 tablespoon cold water
Fresh parsley, finely chopped

Preheat oven to 350°. Rinse sauerkraut in water and squeeze dry. Place in a buttered baking dish. Add beer. Coat one side of ham slices with mustard. Place ham, mustard side *down*, on sauerkraut, overlapping the slices. Sprinkle with raisins and brown sugar. Spot surface with butter. Bake for 30 minutes. Pour liquid from the baking dish into a saucepan and add cornstarch to thicken it into a sauce. Pour sauce over the ham. Garnish with parsley. Serves 2.

BEER AND ONION PANCAKES

1 onion, chopped
1 tablespoon butter
1 cup all-purpose flour

1 pinch salt
1 teaspoon baking powder
1 egg, lightly beaten
1 cup beer
2 tablespoons melted butter or light cooking oil

Sauté onion in butter until lightly browned. Stir flour with salt and baking powder in a bowl. Add egg, beer, and melted butter. Stir in onions. Allow batter to stand 15 minutes before using. Spoon onto well-greased, hot griddle. Makes 10 pancakes.

CHEESE AND BEER SOUFFLÉ

2 tablespoons butter
3 tablespoons flour
1 cup beer
6 eggs, separated
½ cup grated Swiss cheese
¼ cup grated Parmesan cheese
1 dash cayenne pepper
1 pinch nutmeg
1 pinch salt
⅛ teaspoon cream of tartar

Preheat oven to 375°. Line a soufflé dish with waxed paper. Butter the top half of the waxed paper and inside of soufflé dish. Sprinkle with a little Parmesan cheese. Melt 2 tablespoons butter, add the flour, and cook together for 1 minute. Stir in the beer gradually with a wire whisk to form a medium sauce. Add 4 egg yolks and then the grated cheese, pepper, and nutmeg. Beat 6 egg whites with salt and cream of tartar until they stand in soft peaks. Stir 1 cup egg whites into cheese mixture. Then fold cheese mixture into remaining egg whites. Transfer to preheated oven and bake for 25 minutes. Serves 4.

Beer in the Hair and Garden

There are two more things you can do with beer when you're tired of drinking it and cooking with it. I can vouch for the first; the second is hearsay.

Beer was probably the original protein hair conditioner. In fact, you can now buy it in an aerosol can. It's called Charmaine Beer Foam Hair Set and Conditioner. It contains maltodextrins and proteins, just as beer does. It works pretty well, applied after shampooing. But *good* beer works better. I say good beer because it is apt to contain more dextrins and proteins; a German light lager is about right, being not too alcoholic. Just use the beer as a rinse. Set your hair and let it dry. Comb out if you wish. There is no odor after the beer dries. Keep the beer capped and in the refrigerator between shampoos. You'll probably get several treatments out of one bottle, and realize quite a saving over the drugstore products, which aren't half as good as their advertising.

There is a beer shampoo on the market, but it's a waste of money: the detergent in it washes the conditioners right out when you rinse. And that goes for all shampoos that contain so-called protein conditioners. You've got to leave the protein in the hair for a while so that it can do its work, and in most commercial conditioners they use only protein "derivatives," anyway.

The other thing you can do with beer is just for laughs, unless you are a serious gardener who will leap at anything to keep slugs away from the produce. A dear old lady, who gives me beautiful lettuce and tomatoes every year, puts a couple of saucers of beer in the garden. She says the slugs just stay away.

They are, of course, holding out for Pilsner Urquell.

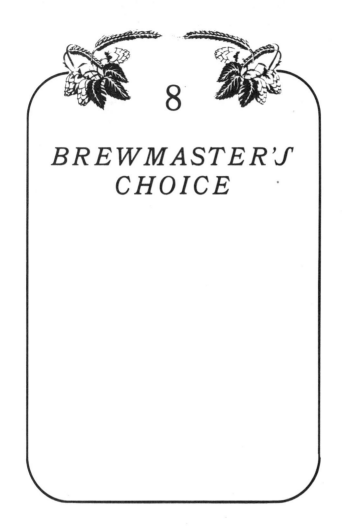

8

BREWMASTER'S CHOICE

WE AMERICANS are no longer a provincial people; we are, indeed, cosmopolitan consumers of many things: imported cars, clothes, liquors, wines, typewriters, and, more and more, beers and ales. The dollar situation may slow up our discovery of the world's bounty, but it probably won't stop it; we've had a taste of honey. We have learned that no single nation makes the best of everything, and we are going to enjoy the best of each if we can.

Now, just because this writer holds a certificate from the United States Brewer's Academy, and has scrubbed a few copper kettles in his day, doesn't mean he's going to try to dictate the brand of beer you should drink. He may know how good beer should be made, but when the potato chips are down, the beer you like is the beer for you. *Don't* just drink it out of habit, though. Habit is a strong thing; it can cut you off from many of life's finest experiences. Here are some brews that this beerman considers to be among the best of their types (not listed in order of preference).

Canada
LeBatt ale
Molson's ale
Moosehead ale
Schooner ale

Czechoslovakia
Pilsner Urquell

Denmark
Carlsberg
Tuborg*

England
Watney's Stingo ale
Mackeson's stout
Watney's Red Barrel beer
Whitbread's Pale ale

France
Kronenbourg (Strasbourg)
La Brasserie Porter 39
Tigre bock (Strasbourg)

---

* Tuborg is also brewed in the United States. Not quite the same, but pretty good.

Germany
Dortmunder Union
Löwenbräu dark
Wurtzburger

Ireland
Guinness stout
Harp

Israel
Maccabee

Japan
Kirin

Mexico
Carta Blanca

Netherlands
Amstel
Grolsch
Heineken

Norway
Ringnes Special

United States
Ballantine India Pale and XXX ales
Budweiser
Coors (Colorado)
Maximus malt liquor
Michelob
Point Special (Wisconsin)
Rheingold (New York)
Schmidt's (Philadelphia)
Stroh's (Detroit)

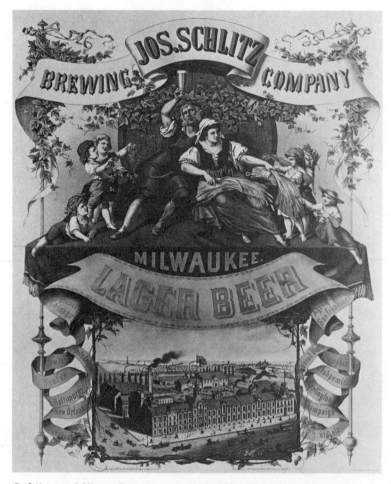

Schlitz of Milwaukee. Joseph E. Schlitz Brewing Company.

A Few Beer-tistics for Those
Who Like to Keep Their Figures

BREWERS REGARD THEIR SALES FIGURES as sacred and secret. But since the federal government collects nine dollars per barrel, it takes a different view of the matter. Here are the top ten sellers of 1972:

1. Anheuser-Busch, Inc. (Budweiser, Budweiser malt liquor, Michelob, Busch Bavarian)—26,552,000 barrels
2. Joseph Schlitz Brewing Company (Schlitz, Schlitz malt liquor, Old Milwaukee, Primo, Encore, Red, White and Blue)—18,906,000 barrels
3. Pabst Brewing Company (Pabst, Blue Ribbon malt liquor, Andeker Supreme, Eastside lager)—12,600,000 barrels
4. Adolph Coors Company (Coors)—9,785,000 barrels
5. Falstaff Brewing Company (Falstaff, Krueger, Narragansett, Ballantine ale and beer)—6,200,000 barrels
6. F. & M. Schaefer Brewing Company (Schaefer)—5,530,000 barrels
7. Miller Brewing Company (Miller High Life, Gettelman, Miller malt liquor, Meister Brau, Lite)—5,400,000 barrels
8. Stroh Brewing Company (Stroh's)—4,231,000 barrels
9. Carling Brewing Company (Black Label, Red Cap ale, Heidelberg beer, ale, and light pilsner, Canadian Gold, Carlsberg, Stag, Tuborg)—4,200,000 barrels
10. Theodore Hamm Company (Hamm's, Waldech, Burgermeister)—3,800,000 barrels

Largest Brewery

ANHEUSER-BUSCH, St. Louis, has 5,000 employees and a production capacity of 9,700,000 barrels per year at this largest of its nine plants.

Smallest Brewery

STEAM BEER BREWERY, San Francisco, has five employees and a production capacity of 10,000 barrels per year.

Worst Brewers

THE MILWAUKEE BREWERS finished fifth in the Eastern Division of the American League in 1973, racking up a 74–88 record. They ended the season 23 games out of first place.

What Nation Rolls Out the Most Barrels?

THE UNITED STATES, OF COURSE: 131,800,000 barrels in 1972, about as much as that pumped out by the next two leading producers—Germany and England—combined. The rest follow (in order): Russia, Japan, Czechoslovakia, France, Canada, East Germany, Australia, Mexico.

How Much Foreign Beer Do We Drink?

EVEN THOUGH we regularly import some ninety brands, foreign beer consumed is only about .7 per cent of the total. And yet we manage to run up an astonishing beer deficit—we import about fourteen times more than we export. The rest of the world seems curiously indifferent to the Old World goodness of our brew. What do they know?

Have You Had Your 19.4 Gallons This Year?

No? Then you're not the typical American beer drinker. Which is to say that you're not a male between the ages of

This German stein, featuring a Teutonic wedding in a Wagnerian setting, towers four feet and holds nine gallons. It has been a center decoration in Luchow's restaurant for almost a century. National Association of Brewers.

twenty-one and thirty-four, you don't live in a Midwestern city, and you're not a member of the upper class. How do you feel now?

And Where Do They Drink the Most Beer—Per Capita?

GERMANY? Wrong! The Northern Territory of Australia, that's where! Sixty U.S. gallons a year is the estimate of what those folks out back drink. Who wouldn't?

Who Made the Strongest Brew?

THOMAS HARDY'S ALE, brewed in July 1968 by the Dorchester Brewery in Dorset, England, was 12.58 per cent by volume. So saith the *Guinness Book of Records.*

And Who Drank the Most the Fastest?

LAWRENCE HILL, twenty-two, of Bolton, Lancashire, England, bolted a 2½-pint yard of ale in 6.5 seconds on December 17, 1964. And a Merry Christmas to all.

And Who Eats the Leftovers?

BREWING extracts only about 65 per cent of the nutrients in the grains it uses. The remainder is salvaged in the brewhouse and goes back to the farmers as feedstuffs containing most of the protein of the original grains. If your chicken tastes like Schlitz, you know who to blame.

What Have They Done for Us Lately?

THE AMERICAN BREWING INDUSTRY is the nation's fourth largest federal excise tax payer, dropping over $1,000,000,000 into the U. S. Treasury every year. Another $400,000,000 goes into state coffers and an undetermined amount into local taxes.